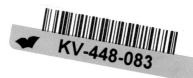

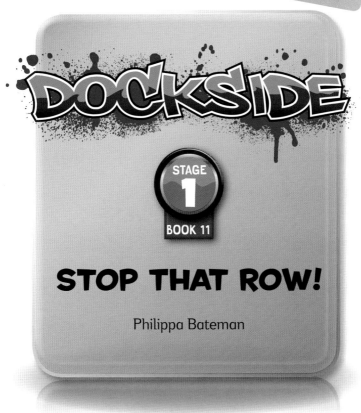

DOCKSIDE

STAGE **1**

BOOK 11

# STOP THAT ROW!

Philippa Bateman

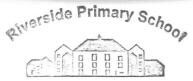

Riverside Primary School

Janeway Street
SE16 4PS
Telephone 020 7237 3227 • Facsimile 020 7237 0047

RISING ★ STARS

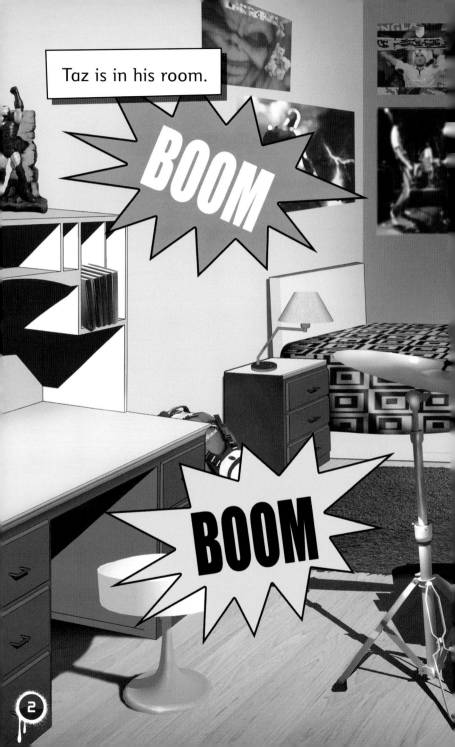

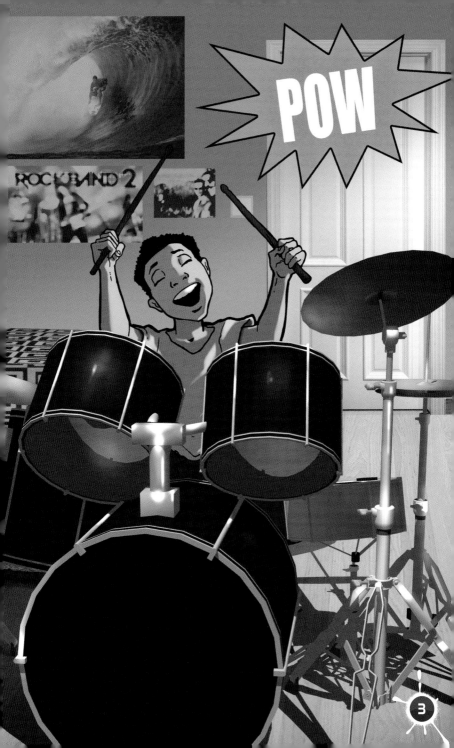

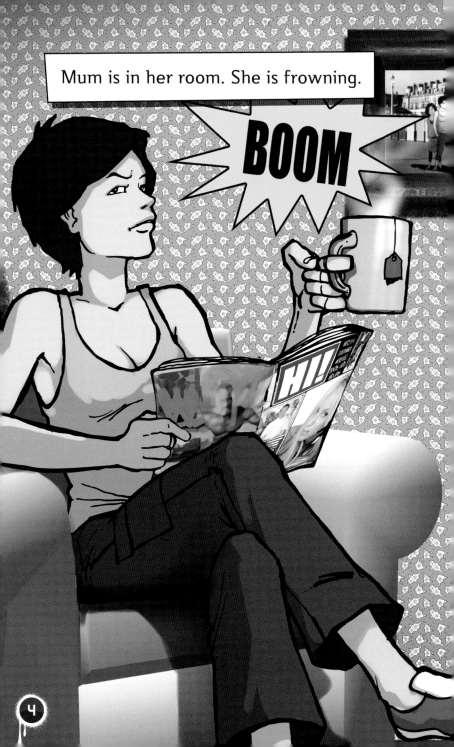

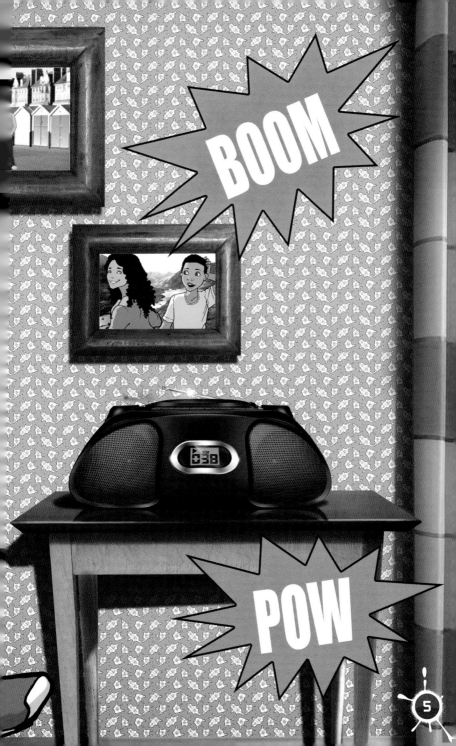

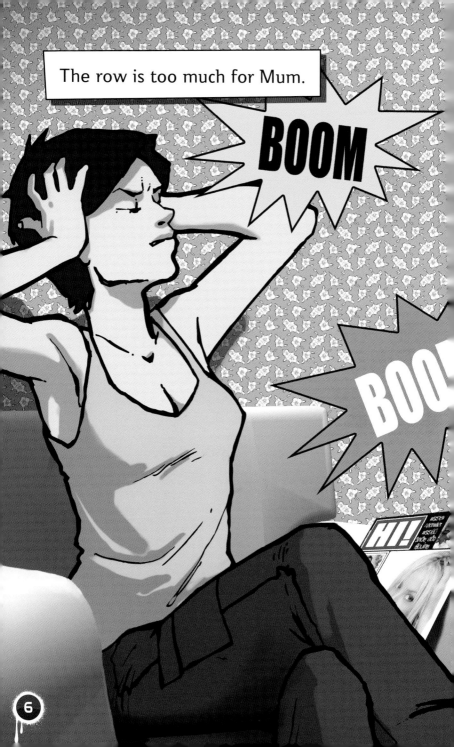

The row is too much for Mum.

BOOM

BOO

HI!

6

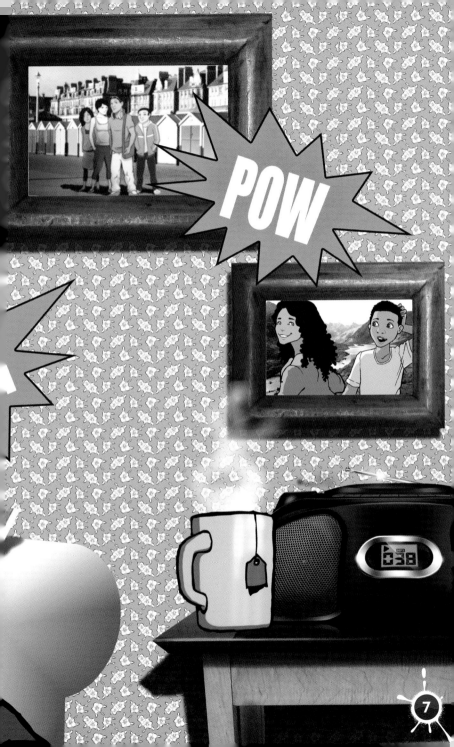

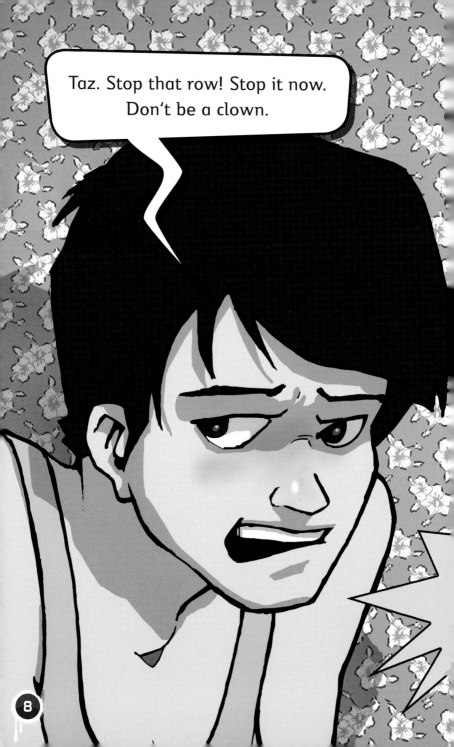

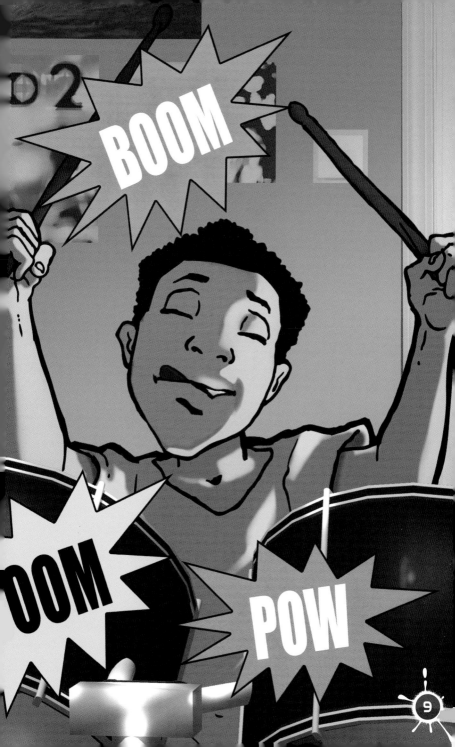

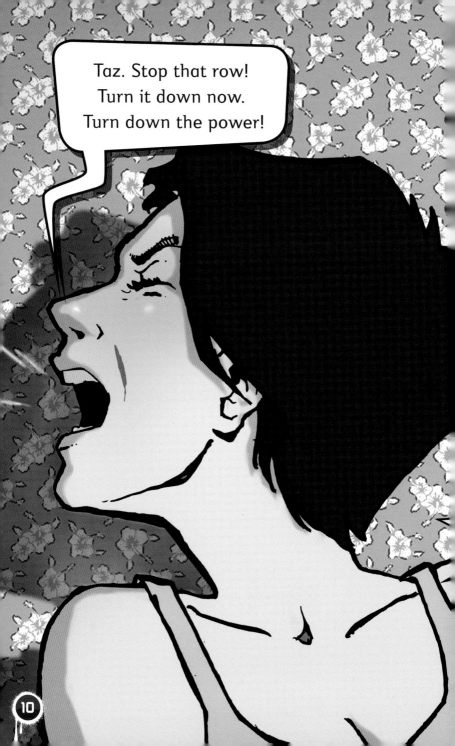

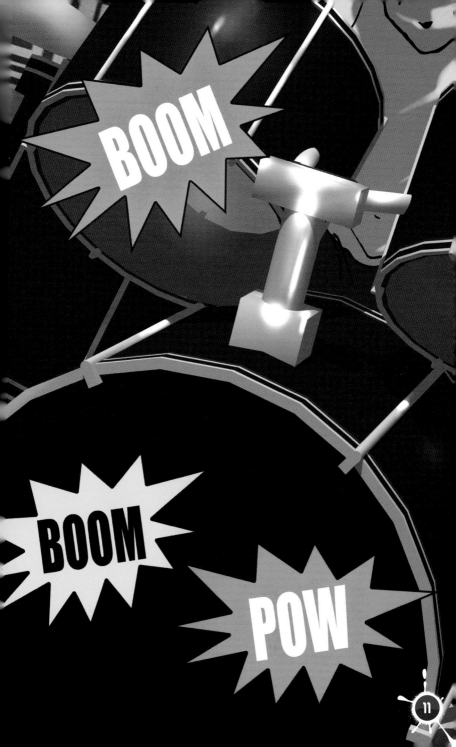

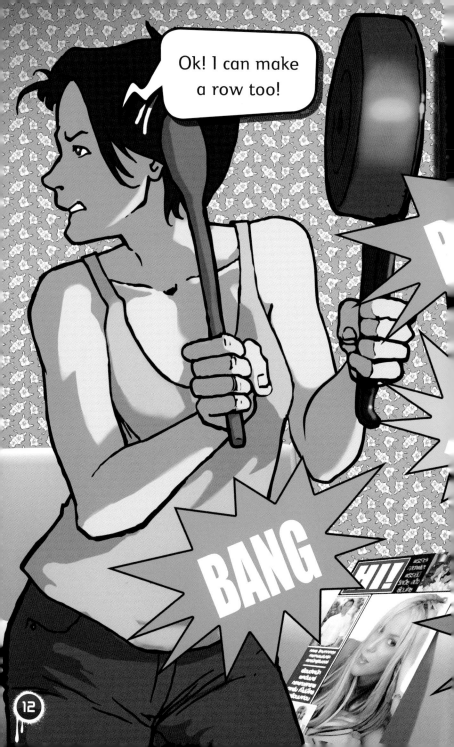

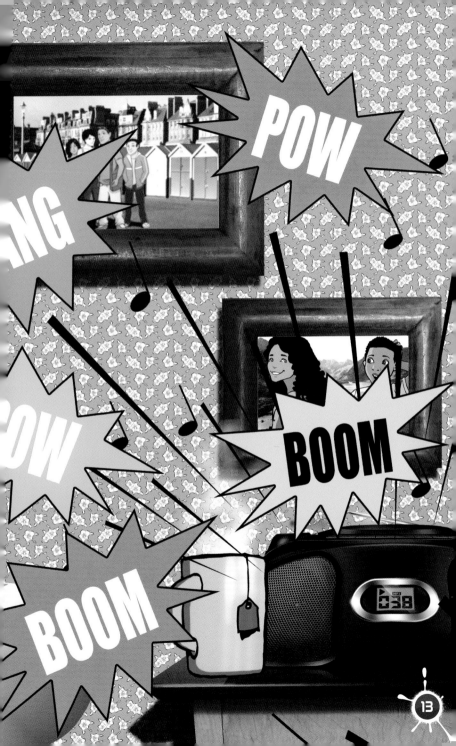

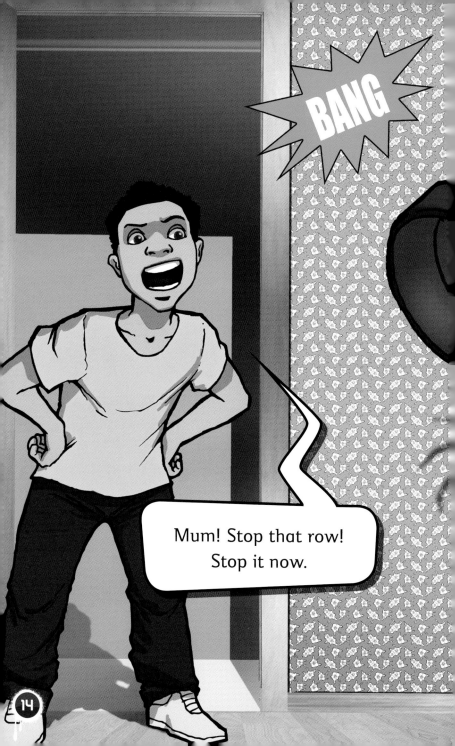

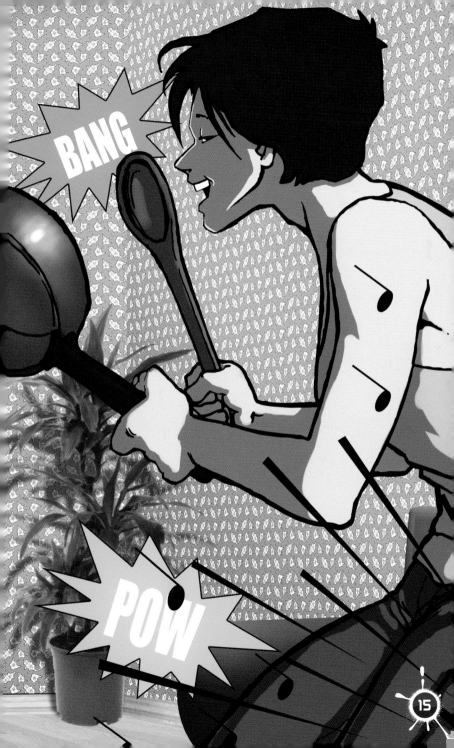

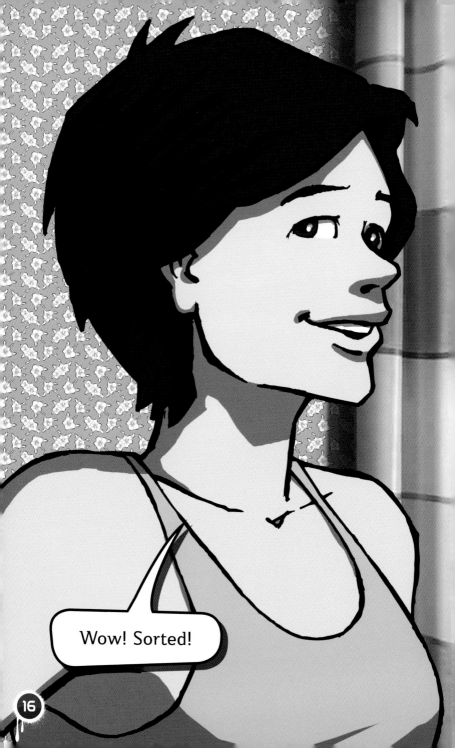